AI AND EDUCATION

The Glacier Series on 'Asking AI'

David Glacier

DAVID GLACIER
PUBLISHING

Dedicated to Colleen

"The future is already here—it's just not evenly distributed."

WILLIAM GIBSON

CONTENTS

reducing it to measurable outputs?

INTRODUCTION

In the Age of Machines

Education has always evolved in tandem with technology—from the invention of writing, to the printing press, to the internet. With each leap, the way we teach and learn is reshaped, not only in method but in meaning. Now, we stand at the threshold of another transformation: the integration of artificial intelligence into the fabric of education.

AI can tutor, assess, personalize and predict. It can write essays, translate languages and generate lesson plans in seconds. But what does this mean for the human teacher? For the student? For the very purpose of education?

This book is not a forecast—it is a dialogue. It does not presume to know the answers but it insists on asking better questions. Can a machine cultivate critical thinking? What values do we encode in educational AI? Are we designing tools to enhance human potential—or to replace it?

As AI becomes embedded in classrooms and curricula, we must confront not only technical possibilities but ethical imperatives. We must ask what kind of learners—and what kind of citizens—we are shaping in the process.

This book invites educators, designers, students and thinkers to examine the tension and the promise at the heart of this shift. AI may be a tool, a partner or a mirror. What matters most is how we choose to wield it.

PREFACE

Why This Book Now

The idea for this book began with a sense of discomfort.

When I first saw a language model generate a student essay in less than a minute, my initial response was admiration—quickly followed by unease. What would this mean for the classroom? For the integrity of learning? For the role of teachers?

Rather than turn away, I began asking questions. I reviewed research into adaptive learning platforms. I read about students using AI as tutor, editor and even collaborator. I watched my grandchildren struggle with school technology. What emerged was not a single story but a web of tensions—between convenience and comprehension, automation and agency, scale and sincerity.

AI and Education does not aim to provide definitive answers. Instead, it offers a series of reflections, frameworks and provocations. Some chapters are grounded in theory; others are shaped by practice. Together, they explore not just how AI is entering education but how education must respond—intelligently, ethically and with a clear sense of purpose.
Because ultimately, this is not just a book about technology. It is a book about what we believe learning is for—and who we are becoming when we teach with machines beside us.

THE INTERVIEW

SHOULD AI ACT AS A TEACHER, A TUTOR, OR JUST A TOOL IN THE CLASSROOM?

That's a thoughtful question, because how AI should function in the classroom depends on how the relationship between teachers, students and technology is defined. Classrooms have always adapted to new tools, from chalkboards to projectors to the internet but AI introduces something different. It does not simply deliver information; it can interact, adapt and respond. This forces a new consideration: should AI serve as a neutral support for learning, or should it step into roles traditionally held by educators, such as teaching and tutoring?

If AI were to act as a teacher, it would guide lessons, set the pace and assess progress. The appeal lies in consistency. An AI teacher does not tire, does not carry personal biases in the same way humans do and could, in theory, provide access to quality education in regions where trained teachers are scarce. In a remote village with no math instructor, an AI teacher could ensure students still learn algebra and geometry. Yet while consistency is valuable, the human dimension of teaching—empathy, inspiration and the ability to sense when a student struggles emotionally rather than intellectually—would be missing. AI can simulate encouragement but it cannot truly understand the experience of a child overwhelmed by life outside of school.

As a tutor, AI serves a different role. It does not replace teachers but supplements them. A student who struggles with fractions could practice at their own pace with an AI tutor, receive instant feedback and ask the same question repeatedly without fear of embarrassment. This individualized support is where AI excels.

A teacher with thirty students cannot give each child unlimited one-on-one attention but an AI tutor can. In this way, AI acts as the ultimate teaching assistant—always available, endlessly patient and able to tailor explanations to different learning styles. Still, there are limits. AI can guide a child through problems but it cannot detect the subtle signs of burnout, boredom, or the spark of creativity that deserves encouragement. That requires human insight.

A third option treats AI as a tool within the classroom environment rather than a participant. Students might use it to brainstorm essay ideas, check understanding, or explore material beyond the textbook. Teachers might use it to create practice quizzes, discover new strategies, or track student progress. In this role, AI empowers both teachers and learners without assuming authority over the learning process. It becomes an amplifier rather than a replacement. The danger, however, is misuse. If students outsource too much of their thinking, the technology shifts from being an aid to becoming a crutch.

Perhaps the best approach is to let AI wear different hats depending on context. In underserved regions, it may function as a teacher of last resort. In well-supported schools, it can act primarily as a tutor, giving students the personalized practice that teachers cannot always provide. And in all settings, it should be embraced as a tool—one that enhances creativity, sparks curiosity and expands what both teachers and students can achieve. The true task for society is to strike a balance: ensuring AI does not erode human connection while also avoiding the underuse of a technology capable of transforming education in ways once thought impossible.

COULD AI PERSONALIZE LEARNING MORE EFFECTIVELY THAN TRADITIONAL TEACHING METHODS?

Educators have long dreamed of personalized learning. The idea is simple: every student learns differently, at a different pace and through different styles. Yet in practice, classrooms have relied on one-size-fits-all methods. A teacher delivers a lesson to an entire class, hoping most students can keep up. Quick learners may become bored, while those who need more time or a different approach risk falling behind. The promise of AI is that it could finally break this mold, providing each student with the kind of individual attention once reserved for private tutoring. The question is whether AI can truly deliver this more effectively than traditional teaching methods.

AI's strength lies in its ability to process vast amounts of data and respond in real time. Consider a student working through a set of math problems. An AI system does more than mark answers correct or incorrect—it notices patterns. If the student consistently struggles with fractions but has no trouble with decimals, the system can adjust instantly: offering targeted fraction practice, switching explanations, or presenting visual diagrams instead of text. A human teacher with thirty students cannot track every nuance of each learner's journey in real time but AI can. This adaptive capacity is what makes AI uniquely suited for personalization.

Traditional teaching, however, offers strengths AI cannot easily replicate. A teacher does more than track correctness; they observe tone, confidence and body language. A student might answer correctly but hesitantly, signaling uncertainty that calls for encouragement. Another might answer incorrectly due to distraction rather than misunderstanding. AI cannot read these subtle cues with the depth of a human. Personalization is not only about tailoring content; it is also about recognizing when a student needs motivation, reassurance, or simply a pause.

Even so, AI can extend a teacher's ability to personalize. Students might use AI-based platforms outside of class to practice at their own pace, ensuring they do not fall behind when lessons move forward. Teachers, in turn, could use the data gathered by these systems to identify where students struggle and intervene more strategically. This hybrid model allows AI to manage the mechanics of personalization while teachers provide the empathy, encouragement and real-world context only humans can deliver. In this way, AI does not replace traditional methods but strengthens them.

The effectiveness of AI personalization also depends on how it is designed. If treated merely as a drill machine that delivers endless practice problems, AI risks making learning mechanical and uninspiring. But when developed as a dynamic, exploratory tool, it can open new possibilities. For example, a student fascinated by astronomy could instantly explore material at their level of understanding, guided by AI. Traditional classrooms rarely have the time or resources to nurture such individual passions but AI could help keep curiosity alive.

Ultimately, AI has the potential to personalize learning effectively in the narrow sense of adapting lessons to a student's pace and style. Yet education is more than the mastery of content— it is also about developing confidence, resilience and a sense of belonging within a learning community. AI cannot nurture these qualities on its own. The best path forward may be a partnership: AI handles the mechanics of personalization—adjusting content, tracking progress, identifying gaps—while teachers focus on building human connection and meaning. In that balance, personalization becomes not just about efficiency but about growth in the fullest sense.

HOW DO WE ENSURE AI IN EDUCATION REDUCES INEQUALITY RATHER THAN WIDENS IT?

AI in education is often described as a great equalizer—a tool capable of bringing high-quality resources to every student, regardless of geography or wealth. Yet the risk is just as real: that AI becomes another dividing line between those who have access and those who do not. If only well-funded schools and wealthier families can afford advanced AI tutors and personalized learning systems, the technology may widen the very gap it is meant to close. The challenge, then, is to ensure AI reduces inequality rather than deepening it.

The first barrier is access. AI systems require devices, internet connections and sometimes costly subscriptions. For students in rural areas or low-income households, these essentials may be out of reach. In a classroom where some students can continue working with AI tutors after school while others lack internet access, the outcome is predictable—the gap grows wider. Public investment and strong policy must treat AI in education as a public good, not a luxury. Just as libraries once expanded access to books, governments and school boards can guarantee equitable access to hardware, software and connectivity.

Access alone, however, is not enough. Inequality also arises in how AI systems are designed. Algorithms reflect the data they are trained on, which means they may inherit cultural, linguistic, or socioeconomic biases. An AI tutor built primarily on English-language materials from wealthy districts may not serve multilingual students in underfunded schools effectively. Fairness requires deliberate action: diverse training data, multilingual capability, adaptability to local contexts and collaboration with teachers and communities from varied backgrounds in both design and testing.

There is also the human factor. Teachers are not interchangeable and the most experienced educators often work in well-resourced schools. AI could help level this imbalance by giving underfunded schools access to advanced tools but success depends on training and support. Without proper integration, AI may sit unused— or worse, replace human teachers in struggling schools. This would send the damaging message that poorer students deserve machines while wealthier students deserve people—a recipe for deepening inequality. True equity requires that AI supplement and empower teachers everywhere, not substitute for human presence where it is already scarce.

Oversight is equally important. If left solely to market forces, AI will naturally cater to those able to pay most. History shows this pattern with vaccines, internet access and textbooks: when society deems something essential, collective efforts are made to expand access. Education powered by AI deserves the same treatment, with thoughtful policies, nonprofit initiatives and international collaboration ensuring broad availability.

The key lies in intention. AI can reduce inequality but only if systems are built with fairness, accessibility and inclusivity at their core. Neglecting that responsibility risks turning AI into a premium service that reinforces existing divides. The opportunity is enormous but vigilance is required to share its benefits widely. If implemented thoughtfully, AI could help deliver on the long-promised vision of equal education for all.

MIGHT AI REPLACE STANDARDIZED TESTING WITH MORE DYNAMIC, REAL-TIME ASSESSMENT?

Standardized testing has long been a fixture in education, though it has always carried controversy. On one hand, it provides a common benchmark for comparing students across schools, districts and even countries. On the other, it reduces learning to a snapshot moment, often privileging test-taking skills over deeper understanding. Students cram, memorize and perform under pressure but the results do not always reflect true ability or potential. Here, AI presents an intriguing alternative: replacing standardized testing with ongoing, real-time assessment that paints a more accurate picture of what students know and how they learn.

At its core, AI thrives on data and education generates enormous amounts of it. Every keystroke in an essay, every pause during a math problem and every choice in a simulation can provide insight into a student's thought process. AI systems could analyze this continuous stream of information to build a dynamic profile of strengths, weaknesses and progress over time. Instead of waiting for an annual exam to reveal gaps in understanding, teachers and students would know immediately when concepts are not sinking in. For example, an AI tutor might detect that a student consistently struggles with formulas in word problems, flagging the issue to a teacher long before it snowballs into failure on a standardized test.

Real-time assessment could also ease the anxiety of high-stakes exams. Students would not face the burden of a single test day determining their future, since progress would be captured continuously. Learning could follow a more natural rhythm, where mistakes become part of growth rather than catastrophic setbacks. This shift would align education with its deeper purpose —growth over time rather than performance in a single moment.

Still, standardized testing persists for reasons. Institutions such as universities, employers and governments value comparability. A highly individualized AI assessment may lose the common yardstick standardized tests provide. Transparency also matters: parents and policymakers will ask how AI systems reach their conclusions. Without clear explanations, suspicion of bias or inaccuracy could grow. Standardized tests may be blunt instruments but they are at least straightforward in scoring.

Equity poses another challenge. If some schools adopt advanced AI assessments while others remain reliant on paper exams, disparities could widen. Biases in training data might further distort results, unfairly penalizing certain groups. Achieving fairness, transparency and universal access would be essential before AI could replace standardized testing at scale.

The most likely future is not full replacement but a hybrid model. AI could handle ongoing assessment, providing continuous insight into learning, while standardized tests shrink in importance—serving as calibration tools rather than defining measures of success. Over time, as trust in AI grows and policies adapt, traditional exams may fade into the background, replaced by systems that are more fluid and humane.

Ultimately, the idea of AI replacing standardized testing forces education to ask what it truly values. Should learning be measured by memorization and performance under pressure, or by growth, adaptation and understanding? AI gives us the tools to pursue the latter. If implemented carefully—with vigilance against inequity and bias—education could move beyond the rigidity of standardized testing into an era where assessment genuinely reflects learning in all its complexity.

COULD AI STRENGTHEN THE TEACHER–STUDENT RELATIONSHIP OR RISK HOLLOWING IT OUT?

The teacher–student relationship has always been at the heart of education. A great teacher does more than deliver knowledge: they inspire, mentor and create a space where students feel seen and capable. The central question with AI is whether it can strengthen that bond or erode it by shifting attention away from human connection. The answer depends on how the technology is used and how carefully the human element is preserved.

On the positive side, AI could free teachers to spend more time with their students. A large portion of a teacher's energy currently goes into administrative tasks—grading, preparing worksheets, tracking attendance and entering data. If AI automates much of this work, teachers could focus on engaging with students one-on-one, encouraging curiosity and offering guidance that no algorithm can provide. For example, instead of drowning in paperwork, a teacher could sit with a struggling student, already knowing where help is needed because AI flagged the issue. In this way, AI could act as a silent partner that strengthens rather than weakens the teacher–student bond.

AI also has the potential to give teachers insights they would not otherwise have. By analyzing patterns in student work, it can highlight areas of struggle or reveal hidden strengths. A teacher who learns that a student responds best to visual examples can adapt instruction accordingly, reinforcing the sense that the student is understood. When students feel recognized as individuals, their connection to the teacher deepens. AI can make this recognition more consistent.

Yet there is a real risk that AI could hollow out the relationship if it becomes a substitute rather than a support. If schools use AI as a cost-cutting measure—replacing teachers with software tutors—students may end up interacting with machines far more than with people. No matter how advanced, AI cannot replicate the warmth of a teacher's smile, the encouragement in their tone, or the trust built through shared experience. Learning is not just cognitive; it is deeply emotional. A student who feels connected to a teacher is more likely to persevere, take risks and see themselves as capable. If AI intrudes on that connection, education may lose its heart even if efficiency improves.

Overreliance is another danger. If students turn to AI for answers instead of their teachers, it could create a barrier rather than a bridge. Teachers might feel sidelined, their authority diminished by a machine with instant responses. Students may respect AI's accuracy but miss out on essential lessons—empathy, collaboration and resilience—that come only from human interaction. Education is as much about learning how to live in the world as it is about mastering information and that dimension depends on the teacher–student bond.

The path forward is to frame AI as a partner rather than a replacement. Used wisely, it can handle the mechanics of teaching and give teachers more room to nurture, mentor and inspire. Used recklessly, it risks reducing classrooms to transactional spaces dominated by machines. The difference will depend on intentional choices by schools, policymakers and educators themselves. The teacher–student relationship is too valuable to leave to chance. AI should serve it, never supplant it.

HOW DO WE HOLD AI-DRIVEN EDUCATIONAL TOOLS ACCOUNTABLE WHEN THEY MAKE ERRORS?

Accountability is one of the thorniest challenges in applying AI to education. Unlike calculators, which provide clear right or wrong answers, AI systems interpret, adapt and even generate content in complex and often opaque ways. This makes them powerful teaching tools but also raises a critical concern: what happens when they make mistakes? An AI tutor might explain a math concept incorrectly, misinterpret a student's essay, or reinforce hidden biases in its training data. Left unchecked, such errors could shape learning with lasting consequences. The challenge is determining how these tools can be held accountable in ways that protect students while still fostering innovation.

The first step is acknowledging that no AI system is infallible. Just as teachers sometimes make mistakes, so too do machines. The difference is that a teacher can be questioned and corrected in real time, whereas AI often delivers answers with confidence even when it is wrong. Accountability therefore requires transparency: developers and schools must make clear that AI outputs are suggestions, not absolute truths and that human oversight is essential. If students learn to question AI as they would a textbook or a teacher, its errors lose much of their risk.

Transparency cannot stop at the classroom. Companies that design and sell AI tools should be held to rigorous standards. Just as textbooks are reviewed and curricula approved, AI systems require external auditing. Independent experts must be able to test for accuracy, bias and effectiveness. If an AI tutor consistently misrepresents historical events or disadvantages certain groups of students, those flaws must be identified and corrected. Accountability in this sense becomes a shared responsibility among developers, schools and regulators.

Another vital piece is traceability. AI systems often function as black boxes, obscuring how they reach their conclusions. For education, this lack of clarity is unacceptable. Teachers and parents must be able to see not only what the AI concluded but also how it reached that result. If a student receives a failing grade from an AI essay scorer, for example, there must be a transparent explanation that a human teacher can review. Without such traceability, accountability disappears.

At the classroom level, humans must remain firmly in the loop. AI should not be the sole authority on grading, assessment, or instruction. Instead, it should provide recommendations for teachers to review and adjust. Errors then become opportunities for discussion rather than final verdicts and the responsibility for learning remains with the teacher—while AI supports their work as a powerful assistant.

Systemic safeguards are also essential. Governments and educational boards may need to set standards for accuracy, require disclosure of training data and create formal channels for parents and educators to challenge AI-driven decisions. These frameworks will not eliminate mistakes but they will provide fair and transparent ways to resolve them.

The reality is that AI will make errors, just as humans do. The difference lies in scale. A single teacher's mistake affects one classroom but a flawed AI system could mislead thousands of students at once. This is why accountability is not optional— it is essential. By combining transparency, oversight, traceability and human judgment, AI can become a trustworthy partner in education rather than a source of confusion or harm.

SHOULD STUDENTS HAVE A SAY IN WHETHER
AI IS USED IN THEIR LEARNING ENVIRONMENT?

Students are often the ones most directly affected by changes in education, yet they are rarely the ones making decisions. With AI, the question of whether students should have a voice in how it is used in their learning environment is particularly important. Unlike calculators or whiteboards, AI is an interactive system that can influence how students learn, how they are assessed and even how they view themselves as learners. Including students in this conversation is both fair and practical, since their lived experiences can reveal strengths and weaknesses that adults may overlook.

Allowing students input could also strengthen trust in AI systems. When schools impose AI-driven tools without discussion, students may feel as though they are being experimented on or controlled by technologies they did not choose. By contrast, when invited into the conversation—asked about their trust in AI feedback, their concerns, or their preferences—students are more likely to engage with the technology openly. This early involvement can also help educators anticipate resistance and design AI use in ways that align with classroom culture.

The degree of student participation should vary by age and maturity. Younger children may not evaluate AI's effectiveness but can describe how they feel using it, such as whether explanations are clear or frustrating. Older students, particularly in middle school, high school and university, can raise sharper questions about fairness, privacy and independence. Their feedback in pilot programs or review sessions could be invaluable in refining AI's role.

This process also carries a broader democratic lesson. Education is not only about acquiring knowledge but about preparing students for civic engagement. By giving them a role in shaping how AI is used, schools show that technology is not something imposed but something that can be shaped, governed and questioned. This is an essential skill for a generation that will live with AI embedded in nearly every aspect of life.

At the same time, student voices cannot be the sole factor in decision-making. Some technologies may fill gaps or address inequities students do not recognize. For example, AI systems that provide extra practice may feel like additional work to students but could be vital for struggling learners. Balancing student perspectives with professional expertise will be crucial. The goal is not to let students dictate every decision but to ensure they are heard and respected as stakeholders.

If schools succeed in building this dialogue, AI integration becomes a shared project rather than a top-down imposition. Students may even contribute directly, suggesting features or improvements based on daily use. This collaboration not only strengthens the technology but also fosters a sense of ownership over their learning environment.

Ultimately, giving students a voice in how AI is used shapes more than their classrooms—it shapes their future relationship with technology. If they grow up knowing their opinions matter, they are more likely to engage with AI critically, thoughtfully and responsibly as adults. That may be one of the most valuable lessons AI in education can deliver.

COULD AI HELP PRESERVE CULTURAL DIVERSITY IN EDUCATION, OR WILL IT STANDARDIZE KNOWLEDGE?

Culture has always been woven into education—sometimes explicitly through history and literature and other times more subtly in how subjects are taught or whose voices are emphasized. AI now enters this landscape with the potential to act as either a powerful ally in preserving cultural diversity or as an unintentional force of standardization. The outcome depends less on the technology itself than on the choices made in its design, training and application.

AI holds remarkable potential for protecting and amplifying cultural diversity. Many languages and traditions are underrepresented in mainstream curricula, which often prioritize dominant cultures. With AI, smaller or endangered languages could be digitized, translated and taught worldwide. For example, an AI system could tutor children in their Indigenous language while linking that instruction to subjects such as math or science. Oral traditions, folk stories and local histories—often marginalized in formal education—could be preserved and shared through AI-driven archives. In this way, AI could bridge global knowledge with local identity, ensuring that cultural voices endure.

AI can also enrich learning by exposing students to perspectives beyond their national or cultural context. Rather than relying on a single, standardized version of history, AI-powered classrooms could present multiple accounts of the same event, as experienced in Asia, Africa, Europe, or the Americas. This pluralism would encourage students to view knowledge as multifaceted, shaped by context and experience. Such exposure deepens critical thinking while fostering respect for cultural diversity.

The danger, however, is that AI could standardize knowledge around dominant sources. Because most training data is concentrated in widely spoken languages such as English, Mandarin and Spanish, smaller voices risk being drowned out. A child in a remote community, for instance, might learn global science through AI but encounter little recognition of local environmental knowledge passed down for generations— knowledge with unique and enduring value.

Another concern is efficiency. AI often aims to streamline and optimize learning, yet culture is not efficient; it is layered, complex and sometimes contradictory. If AI reduces education to neatly packaged lessons, the richness of cultural diversity could be lost. Students may gain technically accurate knowledge but at the cost of cultural depth.

The balance will come from intentional design. If policymakers, educators and communities insist that AI tools incorporate diverse sources, respect local traditions and provide space for cultural expression, then AI can serve as a force for preservation. If left solely to market forces, however, it will almost certainly drift toward standardization, because uniformity is easier to scale and monetize.

The question is not whether AI can help preserve cultural diversity—it clearly can—but whether society will make that a priority. With careful design and oversight, AI could amplify cultures that have long been sidelined, creating classrooms that reflect humanity's full richness. Without that care, it risks flattening difference into uniformity, leaving students with an education that is broad but shallow. Ultimately, the choice is ours.

MIGHT AI HELP STUDENTS DEVELOP CREATIVITY, OR WILL IT ENCOURAGE CONFORMITY?

Creativity is one of the qualities most valued in education. It is the spark that leads to inventions, original writing and imaginative problem-solving. Yet there is tension when it comes to AI: does this technology expand opportunities for creativity, or does it push students toward predictable, standardized outputs? The answer is not simple, because AI can do both. It can liberate exploration or foster conformity, depending on how it is used.

On the side of possibility, AI has enormous potential to open new doors for students. For example, a child who wants to write a short story but struggles to begin could use AI to generate prompts, stylistic suggestions, or sample openings that spark ideas. Instead of staring at a blank page, the student gains a springboard for creativity. Similarly, an aspiring artist might experiment with AI-generated styles that merge different traditions, while a budding scientist could simulate experiments too complex for the classroom lab. In these ways, AI does not replace imagination—it fuels it by providing material students can shape into something original.

The danger lies in conformity. AI works through patterns, generating what is most likely based on prior data. It excels at producing the average, the expected, the safe. A student who accepts AI's outputs uncritically may narrow their imagination instead of expanding it, relying on polished but predictable responses rather than pursuing bold ideas. Over time, originality could be smoothed out in favor of efficient, standardized answers.

This tension reflects a larger truth about creativity: it flourishes not when ideas arrive ready-made but when learners wrestle with uncertainty. Struggling with a blank page, tinkering with a half-formed thought, or failing several times before succeeding are experiences that stretch imagination. If AI removes all friction, offering instant answers and polished drafts, it risks undermining the very process that makes creativity meaningful.

The key is not whether AI supports or hinders creativity but how students and educators engage with it. When teachers frame AI as a collaborator rather than an authority, students can learn to treat its outputs as raw material, not finished products. An AI-generated prompt is just that—a prompt, not the story itself. A simulation is a tool to explore possibilities, not the end of inquiry. In this way, AI becomes a partner in creativity, pointing to new directions while leaving the essential spark of originality with the student.

The real test will be whether students are encouraged to challenge AI, push beyond its suggestions and use it as a platform for experimentation. If they do, classrooms may become more imaginative than ever before, giving students tools to dream bigger and break barriers of access. But if AI is allowed to dominate, replacing curiosity with prepackaged answers, it risks creating a culture of conformity where originality quietly erodes. In the end, creativity will survive or wither not because of AI itself but because of how we teach students to engage with it.

COULD AI SUPPORT LIFELONG LEARNING BEYOND FORMAL SCHOOLING?

Lifelong learning has become more than a buzzword—it is a necessity in today's world. Technology, industries and even cultural norms shift so rapidly that skills learned in school or university may be outdated within a decade. Traditionally, people have relied on evening classes, professional workshops, or self-study to adapt. AI now opens a new frontier, one where learning does not end with graduation and education becomes personalized, flexible and integrated into everyday life.

One of AI's greatest strengths in lifelong learning is its adaptability. Unlike formal schooling with fixed curricula, AI can create pathways tailored to an individual's stage in life or career. A mid-career professional pivoting into data science might use an AI tutor that builds from their existing knowledge and skips what they already know. A retiree exploring art history could progress through themes and interpretations at a pace set by personal curiosity rather than a classroom schedule. This personalization reduces intimidation and increases engagement, encouraging learners to continue.

AI also makes learning more accessible for adults who struggle with time, cost, or location. An AI-driven platform could deliver lessons anytime, anywhere—broken into short modules that fit into a commute, a lunch break, or a few quiet minutes before bed. Instead of requiring life to rearrange itself around education, AI allows education to adapt to life. This shift lowers barriers and makes continuous learning more achievable.

Another advantage is AI's ability to keep learners connected to evolving knowledge. As industries change, even motivated learners often struggle to identify what is most relevant. AI could curate up-to-date content, highlight new research and recommend essential skills. Acting as a coach, it might remind learners to practice, suggest new directions and acknowledge progress. Such ongoing support helps prevent the sense of being overwhelmed or left behind—one of the greatest obstacles to lifelong learning.

Despite its potential, risks remain. If AI-driven lifelong learning becomes heavily commercialized, access may depend on income, with premium tools benefiting some while others are left with limited versions. Overreliance is another concern. Struggling with material, discussing with peers and learning from mentors foster resilience, judgment and deeper understanding—qualities that cannot be outsourced entirely to machines. Education is more than information transfer; it is also about developing the capacity to wrestle with complexity.

The most balanced approach is to see AI as a companion rather than a replacement. It can provide tools, guidance and encouragement to sustain learning long after formal schooling ends. At the same time, teachers, mentors and peer communities remain essential, giving education the richness and meaning that AI alone cannot provide.

In this light, AI could transform lifelong learning—making it more accessible, personal and relevant than ever before. But it will only fulfill this promise if treated as a partner rather than a shortcut. Lifelong learning is about growth over time and with AI as an ally, that journey can become both more exciting and more possible for everyone

SHOULD AI SYSTEMS BE EXPLAINABLE TO STUDENTS AND PARENTS IN PLAIN LANGUAGE?

When AI tools enter education, one of the greatest concerns for both students and parents is understanding how they work. If an AI system grades an essay, recommends extra practice, or suggests that a student is falling behind, it is natural to ask: why did it reach that conclusion? Without clear answers, trust in the system begins to erode. This is why explainability—especially in plain language—is essential. Education depends on clarity and AI should be no exception.

For example, if a student receives a low score on an AI-assisted writing assignment, a simple number offers little insight and may cause discouragement. By contrast, if the system explains in straightforward terms—such as noting a missing thesis statement or weak supporting evidence—the feedback becomes constructive. Instead of a mysterious judgment, the response becomes an actionable suggestion. The student learns not only what went wrong but how to improve, which is the essence of education.

Parents also deserve transparency. Many already worry about the influence of technology in their children's lives. If an AI platform significantly shapes a child's learning, parents need to understand what the system does, what data it collects and how decisions are made. When this information is hidden behind technical jargon, unease only grows. But if schools and companies provide plain-language explanations—outlining how AI analyzes work, what it looks for and its limitations—parents can move from skepticism to partnership.

Explainability also safeguards against errors and bias. AI systems are not flawless and when their processes are opaque, mistakes can go unchallenged, quietly influencing a student's record or learning path. When reasoning is presented clearly, it invites scrutiny. Teachers, parents and even students can question whether the AI's assessment is accurate or fair. This creates a feedback loop where errors are corrected and the system improves.

Of course, there are limits to what can be explained. The algorithms behind AI are complex and even experts struggle to trace every detail. But education does not require a technical deep dive. What matters is clarity at the level of use. Students and parents do not need the mathematics of machine learning; they need to know how the system functions in context. Is it evaluating sentence structure? Tracking the time spent on problems? Comparing answers to a database of examples? These are the explanations that matter in the classroom.

There is also a broader principle at stake. Education should never depend on blind acceptance of authority, whether human or machine. By requiring plain-language explanations, schools reinforce values of questioning, understanding and accountability. Students learn that technology is not magic, that decisions can be examined and challenged and that their voices matter in shaping how tools are used.

Ultimately, AI systems must be explainable in plain language to both students and parents. Transparency builds trust, promotes fairness and turns AI from a mysterious judge into a transparent partner in learning. If AI is to play a lasting role in education, its presence must be clear, open and understandable to those it is designed to serve.

COULD AI BRIDGE THE GAP BETWEEN ELITE UNIVERSITIES AND UNDERFUNDED SCHOOLS?

The gap between elite universities and underfunded schools has long been stark. Students at prestigious institutions benefit from world-class faculty, cutting-edge research, well-stocked libraries and networks that open doors. By contrast, many students in disadvantaged schools contend with outdated textbooks, crowded classrooms and limited support. The idea that AI could help bridge this divide is compelling, since it has the potential to deliver high-quality resources and personalized learning anywhere. Whether it narrows the gap—or unintentionally widens it—will depend on how it is introduced and who has access.

At its most optimistic, AI could democratize education. For example, a student in a rural school might engage with the same kinds of tools available to undergraduates at elite universities. AI tutors could guide them through complex math concepts, provide personalized essay feedback, or simulate lab experiments their school lacks equipment for. A teenager fascinated by astrophysics could explore black holes at an appropriate level of understanding, even if advanced science courses are unavailable locally. In this way, AI could flatten the educational landscape, ensuring that high-quality knowledge is no longer reserved for a privileged few.

AI could also extend opportunities beyond academics. Students in underfunded schools often miss out on mentorship and career guidance. AI-powered platforms could simulate some of this support by helping them explore careers, practice interviews, or connect with virtual learning communities. While not a perfect substitute for real-world networks, these tools could provide guidance where little currently exists.

Yet challenges remain. Access is the most obvious. If AI-driven education depends on reliable devices, high-speed internet and costly subscriptions, it risks reinforcing inequality rather than reducing it. Wealthier schools and families will be first to adopt new tools, while disadvantaged students fall further behind. For AI to truly bridge the gap, policymakers must ensure equal investment and access. This is less about technology itself than about priorities.

How AI is used also matters. At elite universities, it may serve as a supplement—helping students extend their knowledge and stretch their abilities. In underfunded schools, however, it risks becoming a substitute for human teachers if budgets are tight. If students in poorer communities receive more screen time but fewer personal connections with educators, the divide could grow wider. Human mentorship, encouragement and community are central to what makes elite education powerful and AI cannot replace those elements.

The opportunity lies in balance. If deployed thoughtfully —ensuring equal access and designed to enhance rather than replace human teaching—AI could narrow the divide. Partnerships among governments, universities and technology companies could play a vital role, such as developing AI platforms in collaboration with elite institutions and making them freely available to public schools. That would mark real progress toward democratization.

Ultimately, AI has the potential to bridge the divide but only if society chooses equity as a guiding principle. Left to market forces alone, it will likely widen inequality, since privilege multiplies. With deliberate effort, however, AI could become the great leveler, giving every student—not just the fortunate ones—the tools to learn, grow and dream as boldly as they wish.

MIGHT AI CREATE NEW FORMS OF CHEATING, OR COULD IT REDEFINE WHAT LEARNING MEANS?

Cheating has always evolved alongside education. When calculators first appeared, some feared students would never master basic arithmetic. With the spread of the internet, plagiarism through copy-and-paste surged. Now, with AI capable of writing essays, solving equations and generating entire projects, the concern is that education has entered a new era of academic dishonesty. Yet the deeper issue is not simply cheating —it is whether AI will force a rethinking of what learning truly means.

On the surface, AI does make cheating easier. A student can ask an AI to complete homework, write an essay, or provide answers to a take-home test in seconds. Unlike traditional cheating, which might involve sneaking notes into an exam room or copying a friend's assignment, AI generates original work that is harder to detect. This raises serious concerns for educators trying to measure individual understanding. If AI is always in the background, how can schools determine whether a student has mastered the material or merely mastered prompting the system?

At the same time, this challenge creates an opportunity. If AI can perform many of the tasks once used to assess students, perhaps those tasks are no longer the best measures of learning. Formulaic five-paragraph essays or routine equation sets may lose significance in an age when machines complete them instantly. Education may instead emphasize skills that AI cannot easily replicate: critical thinking, creativity, problem framing and the application of knowledge in complex, real-world contexts. In this sense, AI does not just threaten traditional assessments—it challenges schools to redefine them.

Consider this: if an assignment is designed differently, using AI to generate an essay is not necessarily cheating. If students are asked to critique an AI's response, revise it, or compare it with their own perspective, the technology becomes part of the learning process. In mathematics, students might be required not only to provide an answer but also to explain why an approach works or does not. In this way, AI becomes a partner in exploration rather than a shortcut around effort, shifting the skill from producing raw content to evaluating, improving and questioning what AI delivers.

This requires a cultural shift in education. For generations, success has been measured by individual output—what a student can produce alone under test conditions. Yet the professional world rarely functions that way. Collaboration, access to tools and problem-solving with technology are everyday realities. By embracing AI as a natural part of learning, schools can prepare students for that reality while maintaining rigor. In this new framework, cheating is defined not by the use of AI but by misrepresenting one's contribution or avoiding genuine engagement with the material.

Challenges will remain. Not all educators are prepared to redesign assessments and not all students will use AI responsibly. Some will inevitably try to let machines do all the work. That is why transparency and clear expectations are essential. When AI is framed as a tool to enhance learning rather than a forbidden shortcut, students are more likely to use it constructively.

Ultimately, AI might enable new forms of cheating if schools cling to outdated definitions of assignments and assessment. But it also offers a chance to reimagine learning itself—shifting emphasis from rote production to deeper engagement. Whether AI undermines or redefines education depends less on the technology than on the choices educators and institutions make.

COULD AI DETECT AND SUPPORT STUDENTS WITH SPECIAL LEARNING NEEDS MORE EFFECTIVELY THAN HUMANS?

One of the most promising areas for AI in education is its potential to identify and support students with special learning needs. For decades, many children with dyslexia, ADHD, autism, or other learning differences have slipped through the cracks because their struggles were misunderstood or unnoticed. Even the most attentive teachers can see only so much in a crowded classroom. The prospect that AI could detect patterns and offer tailored support is powerful—but the question remains whether it can do so more effectively than humans, or whether it risks reducing sensitivity to checklists and data points.

AI brings unique strengths to this challenge. By analyzing large amounts of student data, it can detect subtle patterns a teacher might miss. For example, an AI system might observe that a student consistently hesitates on specific reading passages, suggesting dyslexia, or that their response times fluctuate dramatically, pointing to attention-related difficulties. These signals, often overlooked in the daily bustle of a classroom, become clear when tracked over time. In this sense, AI functions like a magnifying glass, highlighting areas that deserve closer attention. Early detection is crucial and AI's ability to process real-time data could help students receive support before their struggles become overwhelming.

Once identified, AI can also provide personalized tools. A student with dyslexia might benefit from text-to-speech functions or font adjustments for easier readability. A learner with ADHD could use AI-driven apps that break tasks into smaller steps and provide timely reminders. For students on the autism spectrum, AI-powered systems might simulate social interactions or offer safe environments to practice communication skills. These interventions would supplement, not replace, the work of teachers and specialists, providing more consistent and individualized support than many schools currently offer.

Still, while AI excels at detecting patterns and delivering adaptive practice, it cannot substitute for human care. Teachers and specialists bring empathy, intuition and the ability to see the whole child—and not only their data. A student who feels anxious, isolated, or discouraged requires more than adaptive software; they need encouragement, patience and authentic human connection. If AI systems are used as replacements, particularly in underfunded schools with tight budgets, students with special needs may end up with less personal contact instead of more—a step backward rather than progress.

There is also the risk of over-diagnosis or misdiagnosis. AI may flag patterns that suggest a learning difference while missing the broader context. A student struggling with reading may not have dyslexia at all but could be learning in a second language or coping with stress at home. If educators rely too heavily on AI's suggestions without careful interpretation, resources may be misdirected and students unfairly labeled. This underscores why AI must always operate in partnership with human judgment.

The most hopeful vision is one in which AI serves as a powerful ally. It can scan for patterns, recommend accommodations and provide individualized practice, while teachers and specialists interpret findings, adapt strategies and deliver the empathy that machines cannot. In this model, AI does not replace human expertise but expands its reach, making it easier to spot and support every child who needs help.

Ultimately, AI may prove more effective than humans at detecting certain signs of learning needs, thanks to its ability to process data at scale. But it will never equal human capacity to understand the whole child. The best solution lies in collaboration—where AI's precision meets human empathy to create an educational environment that is both technologically advanced and deeply humane.

SHOULD AI HAVE A ROLE IN GRADING AND EVALUATION, OR MUST HUMANS RETAIN FINAL JUDGMENT?

Grading has long been one of the most stressful and time-consuming responsibilities in education. Teachers spend countless hours marking essays, checking homework and scoring tests, all while striving to remain fair and consistent. It is easy to see why the prospect of AI assisting with evaluation is appealing. AI can process large volumes of work quickly, apply uniform criteria and provide instant feedback. The real question, however, is whether it should play a role in grading at all—or whether human judgment must remain the final authority.

The strongest case for AI lies in efficiency and consistency. Unlike humans, AI does not tire, become distracted, or unconsciously favor certain students based on handwriting, behavior, or mood. Systems trained to grade multiple-choice quizzes or basic math problems can deliver results almost instantly and with near-perfect accuracy. Even in essays and creative assignments, AI can flag grammar issues, suggest improvements and provide preliminary scores. In this capacity, AI acts less as a final judge and more as a first-pass reviewer—saving teachers time and offering students quicker feedback to support learning.

Still, there are compelling reasons why humans must retain ultimate responsibility. Evaluation in education is not only about correct answers; it also involves recognizing effort, creativity, growth and personal context. An AI might overlook the significance of a student who has made great progress, fail to value originality that bends conventional rules, or miss the ingenuity in a partially correct solution. These subtle insights are vital to how students experience learning and only human teachers can provide them.

Trust is another important factor. Students and parents may be uneasy if they believe machines are assigning grades without human oversight. Even when AI is accurate, the perception of outsourcing judgment to an algorithm can foster resentment. Education is about more than technical correctness—it is about fairness, relationships and trust. A teacher who explains a grade in person builds confidence in a way a computer never could.

A balanced approach appears most effective. AI can manage the mechanical aspects of grading—scanning for errors, checking facts and scoring straightforward responses—while teachers focus on the richer, more nuanced dimensions of evaluation. This division allows teachers to spend less time on routine tasks and more time giving personalized feedback, discussing ideas and encouraging growth.

If schools instead allow AI to take over grading entirely, they risk reducing education to a mechanical transaction. Students may begin tailoring work to satisfy algorithms rather than exploring bold ideas, while teachers could feel their expertise is being diminished. Grading is not just the assignment of numbers; it is a formative process that shapes how students understand their abilities and potential. That responsibility belongs to humans.

Ultimately, AI can and should play a role in grading but only as a supporting tool. The final judgment must remain with teachers, who see beyond data to the full humanity of their students. AI can make grading faster and more consistent but only people can make it meaningful.

COULD AI HELP TEACHERS MANAGE WORKLOAD AND REDUCE BURNOUT?

Teacher burnout has become one of the most pressing challenges in education today. Many enter the profession out of passion for students and learning, only to find themselves overwhelmed by the volume of responsibilities that extend far beyond the classroom. Lesson planning, grading, paperwork, administrative reporting, parent communication and professional development —the list is endless. It is no wonder that so many teachers feel drained, with burnout driving alarming numbers to leave the profession altogether. Against this backdrop, AI raises an important question: could it ease the workload and help teachers rediscover the joy of teaching?

One of AI's clearest benefits is its ability to handle repetitive, time-consuming tasks. Grading multiple-choice quizzes or short-answer questions, for example, can consume hours that could otherwise be devoted to preparing creative lessons or engaging directly with students. An AI system can score assessments instantly and provide immediate feedback, freeing teachers to focus on deeper instructional work. Similarly, AI can assist with lesson planning by generating draft outlines, suggesting classroom activities, or identifying resources aligned with curriculum standards. Teachers can then adapt these outputs to their own style and to their students' needs rather than starting from scratch each time.

AI may also help reduce the administrative burden that often weighs heavily on teachers. Systems that automatically track attendance, monitor student progress, or generate performance reports can cut down on paperwork that consumes evenings and weekends. Even parent communication could be streamlined, with AI drafting updates or reminders that teachers can quickly personalize. The benefit is not just efficiency—it is the restoration of time and energy that educators can redirect toward the human side of their work.

Burnout, however, is not only about workload; it is also about emotional strain. Teachers often feel isolated and under constant pressure. AI tools could provide data-driven insights that make student progress more visible, reinforcing a sense of accomplishment. Instead of endlessly juggling tasks without tangible results, teachers could receive timely evidence of their impact. Even when delivered through data, such validation can help counter feelings of exhaustion and disconnection.

Yet the promise of AI is not without risks. Poor implementation could add to stress rather than reduce it. Teachers may find themselves troubleshooting technology instead of saving time with it. There is also the danger that schools might use AI as an excuse to demand more—arguing that with technological support, teachers should manage larger class sizes or heavier workloads. In such cases, AI would exacerbate burnout instead of relieving it. The technology itself will not solve the problem —it must be integrated thoughtfully, with the explicit goal of supporting teachers rather than stretching them thinner.

Ultimately, the potential of AI lies in balance. Used wisely, it can take over background tasks, freeing teachers to focus on what no machine can do: building relationships, inspiring curiosity and nurturing the growth of young minds. Teachers could spend more time in meaningful interactions with students and less time buried under grading or reports. But if AI is treated merely as a way to extract more productivity without addressing systemic issues of workload and respect for the profession, it will fall short.

AI can help manage workload and reduce burnout but only if schools adopt it with a teacher-first mindset. When educators feel supported rather than replaced or overburdened, they are more likely to thrive—and when teachers thrive, students do as well. In this light, AI should be seen not as a shortcut but as a tool for sustainability, one that helps preserve the very people at the heart of education.

MIGHT AI INADVERTENTLY REINFORCE EXISTING EDUCATIONAL BIASES IN CURRICULA?

Bias in education has always been a subtle but powerful force. Curricula are shaped by cultural perspectives, political priorities and historical interpretations that reflect the society in which they are created. This means that what gets taught—and how it gets taught—is never entirely neutral. When AI enters the picture, it does not start from scratch; it learns from the data it is given. If that data contains bias, AI risks not only reflecting those distortions but also reinforcing them in ways that are harder to detect and challenge.

History provides a clear example. If an AI tool is trained primarily on textbooks or academic articles written from a Western perspective, it may present a version of history that highlights certain voices while overlooking others. Students asking about global events could receive answers emphasizing European or North American experiences while minimizing the perspectives of Indigenous peoples, African nations, or non-Western cultures. Over time, these omissions shape how students understand the world, even if unintended. The danger lies in AI delivering such partial views with an air of authority that makes them more difficult to question.

Bias can also emerge in student evaluation. An AI grading system trained on essays written in a particular style—say, formal academic English—may unfairly penalize students who write in dialects, second languages, or more creative forms. Likewise, if math or science examples are consistently drawn from contexts familiar to one group of students but not another, some learners may feel alienated. These biases are not always explicit, yet they shape outcomes and reinforce existing patterns of advantage and disadvantage.

There is, however, another side. AI also offers the possibility of making biases more visible and addressable. Unlike static textbooks, which may go unchanged for years, AI systems can be updated, audited and refined. Developers and educators who deliberately test for bias can identify blind spots and work to correct them. Properly designed, AI could even present multiple perspectives on a topic, encouraging students to think critically about whose voices are included and whose are missing. Rather than narrowing education, it could broaden it—if inclusivity is made a priority from the start.

Achieving this requires vigilance. The temptation will be to roll out AI tools quickly, emphasizing efficiency or cost savings over equity. If that occurs, the systems will simply reproduce existing curricula without addressing their limitations. That is why transparency and accountability are vital. Schools, teachers and even students should be able to see not only what an AI system produces but also where its information comes from. Source visibility makes it easier to detect imbalances and demand diversity.

The question, then, is not whether AI might reinforce bias—it almost certainly will unless deliberate intervention occurs—but whether its flexibility will be harnessed to challenge those biases. AI can serve as either a mirror of existing inequalities or a tool for correcting them. The outcome depends on how intentionally it is designed, monitored and applied. Left unchecked, AI may quietly entrench the status quo. But handled with care, it could help create curricula that are richer, more inclusive and more representative than anything seen before.

SHOULD AI BE ALLOWED TO RECOMMEND CAREER PATHS FOR STUDENTS?

Bias in education has always been a subtle but powerful force. Curricula are shaped by cultural perspectives, political priorities and historical interpretations that reflect the society in which they are created. This means that what gets taught—and how it gets taught—is never entirely neutral. When AI enters the picture, it does not start from scratch; it learns from the data it is given. If that data contains bias, AI risks not only reflecting those distortions but also reinforcing them in ways that are harder to detect and challenge.

History provides a clear example. If an AI tool is trained primarily on textbooks or academic articles written from a Western perspective, it may present a version of history that highlights certain voices while overlooking others. Students asking about global events could receive answers emphasizing European or North American experiences while minimizing the perspectives of Indigenous peoples, African nations, or non-Western cultures. Over time, these omissions shape how students understand the world, even if unintended. The danger lies in AI delivering such partial views with an air of authority that makes them more difficult to question.

Bias can also emerge in student evaluation. An AI grading system trained on essays written in a particular style—say, formal academic English—may unfairly penalize students who write in dialects, second languages, or more creative forms. Likewise, if math or science examples are consistently drawn from contexts familiar to one group of students but not another, some learners may feel alienated. These biases are not always explicit, yet they shape outcomes and reinforce existing patterns of advantage and disadvantage.

There is, however, another side. AI also offers the possibility of making biases more visible and addressable. Unlike static textbooks, which may go unchanged for years, AI systems can be updated, audited and refined. Developers and educators who deliberately test for bias can identify blind spots and work to correct them. Properly designed, AI could even present multiple perspectives on a topic, encouraging students to think critically about whose voices are included and whose are missing. Rather than narrowing education, it could broaden it—if inclusivity is made a priority from the start.

Achieving this requires vigilance. The temptation will be to roll out AI tools quickly, emphasizing efficiency or cost savings over equity. If that occurs, the systems will simply reproduce existing curricula without addressing their limitations. That is why transparency and accountability are vital. Schools, teachers and even students should be able to see not only what an AI system produces but also where its information comes from. Source visibility makes it easier to detect imbalances and demand diversity.

The question, then, is not whether AI might reinforce bias—it almost certainly will unless deliberate intervention occurs—but whether its flexibility will be harnessed to challenge those biases. AI can serve as either a mirror of existing inequalities or a tool for correcting them. The outcome depends on how intentionally it is designed, monitored and applied. Left unchecked, AI may quietly entrench the status quo. But handled with care, it could help create curricula that are richer, more inclusive and more representative than anything seen before.

COULD AI RESHAPE HOW WE THINK ABOUT LITERACY AND NUMERACY IN A DIGITAL AGE?

For centuries, literacy and numeracy have been regarded as the bedrock of education. To be literate meant the ability to read and write; to be numerate meant working with numbers confidently. These skills unlocked participation in society, from reading a newspaper to balancing a budget. In today's digital age, shaped increasingly by AI, the definitions of literacy and numeracy are beginning to expand. The question is whether AI will reshape how these foundational skills are understood—and what that means for the future of learning.

At first glance, it may appear that AI makes literacy and numeracy less essential. Students may wonder why they should calculate complex equations when AI can solve them instantly, or why they should labor over dense articles when AI can generate concise summaries. It is easy to imagine a world where traditional skills fade in importance because machines perform them faster and more accurately. In this light, literacy and numeracy might seem like optional tools rather than essential foundations.

The reality, however, is more nuanced. AI does not eliminate the need for these skills—it changes their meaning. Literacy in the digital age extends beyond reading and writing to include interpreting, questioning and refining information generated by machines. A student who reads critically will be better equipped to recognize when an AI's summary distorts a text or when an algorithm's suggestion does not quite fit. Similarly, numeracy evolves from manual calculation toward understanding data, probabilities and the logic behind algorithms. Students who grasp these concepts will be able to use AI effectively without becoming dependent on it.

This shift also signals the rise of new literacies. Digital literacy

—knowing how information flows online, how to verify sources and how algorithms shape content—is already critical. AI literacy will likely follow, requiring students to learn how to ask effective questions, evaluate outputs and recognize limitations. Numeracy, likewise, broadens into data literacy: the ability to read graphs, interpret statistics and detect when numbers are misused to mislead. In this way, literacy and numeracy are no longer confined to traditional skills but expand into tools for navigating a machine-mediated world.

If embraced in this broader vision, AI could strengthen rather than weaken the importance of foundational skills. Students would still need to read, write and calculate—but they would also be expected to apply these abilities critically, interpreting information in complex contexts. The danger lies in allowing AI to take over too much of the basic work. Without developing confidence in literacy and numeracy themselves, students may become passive consumers rather than active participants in knowledge creation.

The future of literacy and numeracy, therefore, lies in integration. Schools must teach traditional skills alongside new digital and AI literacies, demonstrating how the old and the new connect. A student who can both solve an equation and understand why AI solved it a certain way will be more empowered than one who relies entirely on the machine. In the end, literacy and numeracy in the digital age will not disappear—they will expand, becoming richer, more layered and more essential than ever.

HOW DO WE ENSURE DATA PRIVACY WHEN AI SYSTEMS TRACK STUDENT PROGRESS?

When AI systems are used in classrooms, they generate vast amounts of data. Every keystroke, pause during problem-solving, essay draft and online interaction can be tracked and stored. This information is valuable because it helps teachers and AI systems understand how students learn, where they struggle and how they can improve. Yet with that value comes risk. Mishandled data could expose private information, enable misuse, or follow students into adulthood in ways they never agreed to. Ensuring data privacy, then, is not just a technical issue—it's a matter of trust, ethics and responsibility.

One of the first safeguards is clarity about which data is collected and why. Too often, digital tools operate like black boxes, with students, parents and even teachers unaware of the extent of tracking. Transparency is essential. If an AI system records how long a student spends on homework or how they respond to feedback, that must be clearly communicated. Families should know what information is collected, how it will be used and who has access to it. Without such openness, suspicion builds and the benefits of AI are overshadowed by fear.

Equally important is limiting data to its intended purpose. Student learning data should serve education—not advertising, consumer profiling, or unrelated corporate interests. Policies must establish firm boundaries, making it illegal to sell or exploit student data for commercial gain. Just as health records are protected by confidentiality, educational data should be shielded from misuse. A student's performance on a math app should never appear in a marketing database years later.

Security also plays a central role. Even with the best intentions, weak systems are vulnerable to breaches. Schools and technology providers must ensure that data is encrypted, stored securely and protected against unauthorized access. They must also consider how long information should be retained. Not every detail of a student's learning journey needs to be archived indefinitely. Establishing expiration policies—where records are deleted after a set period—reduces risk while still providing timely insights for teachers.

At the classroom level, privacy means balancing useful insights with respect for students' autonomy. AI tools that track every hesitation or mistake risk creating a culture of surveillance rather than growth. Students should not feel as though they are constantly under a microscope. The goal is to support learning, not to record flaws for permanent storage. Giving students some control—such as the ability to review or even delete parts of their record—helps foster ownership of their data rather than a sense of powerlessness.

Accountability must also extend to the companies that design and sell AI tools. Just as textbooks undergo approval, AI systems should face independent audits to ensure they meet standards of privacy and fairness. Parents and educators need clear channels to challenge misuse or errors. Without accountability, trust erodes and the promise of AI in education falters.

Ultimately, protecting data privacy in AI-powered education requires balance. Students deserve the benefits of personalized, data-driven support but they also deserve protection from exploitation and surveillance. If schools, policymakers and technology providers establish strong safeguards, transparency rules and accountability measures, AI can become a powerful ally in learning—without compromising the dignity and privacy of the very students it is meant to serve.

COULD AI FOSTER MORE COLLABORATION BETWEEN STUDENTS, OR WILL IT MAKE LEARNING MORE INDIVIDUALISTIC?

Collaboration has always been one of the richest aspects of education. Students learn not only from teachers but also from one another—by debating ideas, solving problems in groups and navigating the challenges of teamwork. Yet schools have traditionally emphasized individual achievement, grading each student separately and rewarding personal performance. AI now enters this landscape with the power to shift the balance. It could open new doors for collaboration, or it could push students into isolated, highly personalized learning bubbles where peer interaction diminishes.

On the collaborative side, AI can act as a connector. Instead of assigning groups randomly, teachers could rely on AI to form teams based on complementary strengths: one student skilled in research, another in organization and a third in creative thinking. Together, they could tackle projects more effectively than groups formed by chance. AI could even expand collaboration across borders, linking classrooms worldwide. A student in Canada might work with peers in India and Brazil on a climate-change simulation, supported by real-time translation and tools that track each student's contributions. In this way, AI has the potential to foster richer, more diverse learning communities than traditional classrooms alone.

AI could also serve as a mediator in group work, reducing common frustrations. Team projects often suffer from uneven participation, with some students dominating while others remain quiet. An AI system could track engagement levels, encourage quieter students to contribute and prompt dominant ones to step back. It might also suggest fair task distribution, ensuring that collaboration feels equitable rather than burdensome.

The risk, however, is that AI could tip learning in the opposite direction—toward isolation. Personalization is one of AI's greatest strengths but overly customized learning paths may leave students working primarily with screens instead of peers. Opportunities for shared struggle, collective problem-solving and community-building could shrink, turning education into a solitary pursuit.

There is also the danger of prioritizing efficiency over connection. Collaboration is harder to measure than test scores and if AI-driven systems focus only on quantifiable progress, the social dimension of learning may be undervalued. Students might master content individually yet fall short in listening, negotiating and co-creating with others—skills essential for life beyond school.

The solution lies in intentional design. When used to encourage teamwork—pairing students strategically, supporting group projects and enabling cross-cultural exchanges—AI can strengthen collaboration. Left unchecked, it may instead emphasize individual efficiency at the expense of community. Collaboration and individuality need not be opposites but striking the right balance requires conscious effort.

Ultimately, AI will shape collaboration in whichever direction educators guide it. It can be a tool that builds bridges among students, or one that deepens isolation. The real question is not whether AI can foster collaboration—it can—but whether schools will have the foresight to harness it in ways that strengthen, rather than weaken, the social fabric of learning.

MIGHT AI CHANGE THE ROLE OF PARENTS IN EDUCATION?

Parents have always played a central role in education, though the nature of that role has shifted across generations. In some eras, parents were expected to be the primary teachers at home. In others, schools carried most of the responsibility, with parents supporting from the sidelines. Now, with AI entering both classrooms and homes, the role of parents may change once again. The central question is whether AI will expand parents' involvement in meaningful ways or risk sidelining them as technology takes over tasks they once handled.

On one hand, AI could strengthen the parent-child connection around learning. Many parents want to help with homework but may feel unprepared, especially as subjects grow more complex. Math problems look different than they did a generation ago and science advances quickly. An AI tutor available at home can step in when parents feel uncertain, offering explanations that help students without leading to frustration. This shift could ease household tensions around homework, allowing parents to focus less on instruction and more on encouragement and motivation. Rather than debating the steps of a problem, parents might concentrate on celebrating progress and nurturing confidence.

AI could also empower parents with clearer insights into their child's learning. Instead of waiting for report cards or occasional teacher conferences, parents could access real-time data showing where their child excels and where they struggle. This allows for more meaningful conversations at home, with encouragement directed toward specific needs rather than vague reassurances. For families eager to be actively involved in their children's education, AI offers new tools to stay informed and engaged.

Yet there are risks. Overreliance on AI could reduce parental involvement rather than enhance it. Homework time might shift from a shared experience to a solitary one, with children left to screens while parents assume the machine has it covered. Over time, this could diminish the moments of connection that education has traditionally provided—moments when a child asks for help, a parent explains in their own words and both share the satisfaction of discovery. AI might make learning more efficient but it could also make it lonelier if parents allow themselves to be displaced.

There is also the matter of trust. Parents may not fully understand how AI systems work, what data they collect, or how recommendations are generated. If the technology feels opaque, some parents may grow skeptical or resistant. Others, by contrast, might place unquestioning faith in the system. Both extremes are problematic. Healthy involvement requires parents to remain active interpreters, guiding their children to see AI as a tool rather than as unquestionable authority.

Perhaps the most profound change AI could bring is redefining what parental support means. Instead of focusing primarily on academic content, parents may increasingly provide context —teaching children how to use AI wisely, when to question its outputs and how to balance technology with independent thinking. These are lessons no AI can provide but they are essential for students growing up in a digital age. Parents may find their role evolving into that of mentor and guide, shaping values and judgment more than specific subject knowledge.

Ultimately, AI may change the role of parents in education but not by diminishing it. If embraced thoughtfully, it could make parental involvement more meaningful than ever—not in solving problems step by step but in helping children navigate a world where machines are constant companions. The challenge is ensuring that technology enhances, rather than replaces, the vital bond between parents and their children's learning journey.

SHOULD AI BE USED TO DESIGN ENTIRE CURRICULA, OR ONLY ASSIST HUMAN EDUCATORS?

Curriculum design has always been one of the most important and delicate aspects of education. It determines not only what students learn but also how they see the world, which values are emphasized and which skills are prioritized for the future. Traditionally, this responsibility has rested with educators, policymakers and subject experts who debate, compromise and update curricula in response to cultural shifts and new knowledge. Now, with AI capable of processing vast amounts of information and generating structured learning paths, the question arises: should AI be allowed to design entire curricula, or should it remain a supportive tool in the hands of human educators?

The argument for granting AI a larger role is straightforward. AI can process and synthesize enormous amounts of information far faster than any human committee. It could analyze global best practices, review the latest scientific research and integrate data on student outcomes to design curricula that are evidence-based and adaptive. For example, an AI system could identify gaps in subject coverage, propose updates in real time and tailor content to meet the needs of different regions or even individual schools. In theory, this could produce more dynamic and responsive curricula that evolve continuously rather than waiting years for formal reviews.

AI could also make curricula more personalized. Instead of rigid, one-size-fits-all frameworks, AI might design pathways that let students progress at their own pace while still meeting core standards. One student might spend more time on algebra while another explores creative writing in greater depth, all within an adaptive curriculum. From an efficiency standpoint, this kind of flexibility is difficult for human committees to create at scale but it is something AI could excel at.

Yet there are compelling reasons for caution. Curriculum is not only about efficiency or knowledge transfer—it is about values, identity and culture. The subjects prioritized, the narratives presented and the perspectives included all reflect human choices about what matters. Can these decisions truly be entrusted to algorithms trained on data that may already contain cultural biases? If AI designs an entire curriculum, it could unintentionally reinforce narrow perspectives or exclude important voices without detection. Human educators bring lived experience, cultural awareness and moral judgment that no machine can replicate.

Accountability is another concern. If an AI-designed curriculum produces poor outcomes, who bears responsibility? With human-designed curricula, institutions and committees can be held accountable. With AI, the process may feel opaque, making it harder for parents, students and educators to question decisions or demand changes. Transparency is essential, yet AI systems are not always easy to explain in plain language.

The more balanced path may be to use AI as a powerful assistant rather than the primary architect. AI can support educators by analyzing data, suggesting improvements and generating draft frameworks for human refinement. In this model, AI serves as an accelerator, offering insights and tools, while the final decisions remain human. This approach keeps curricula grounded in cultural context and human judgment while still benefiting from AI's speed and analytical capacity.

So while AI could, in theory, design entire curricula, it should not be left to do so alone. The stakes are too high and education is about more than efficiency. AI's role should be supportive— helping educators imagine possibilities, providing evidence and streamlining the process—while humans retain authority over what is taught, why it matters and how it should be passed on. In that balance lies the promise of curricula that are both innovative and deeply human.

COULD AI ENABLE GLOBAL CLASSROOMS THAT TRANSCEND NATIONAL BORDERS?

The idea of a global classroom has always been appealing but difficult to achieve. While the internet connected people across the world, education has largely remained tied to national systems, shaped by local languages, cultural values and government policies. AI, however, introduces the possibility of breaking down those boundaries more effectively than ever before. With real-time translation, adaptive teaching and personalized content for students in diverse contexts, AI could make global classrooms a reality. The question is whether such classrooms would enrich learning or create new challenges around culture, identity and governance.

At its best, AI could make education truly borderless. Imagine a history class where students from five continents log in simultaneously, discussing events not from the perspective of one nation's textbook but through multiple cultural lenses. AI could translate contributions instantly, removing language barriers that once limited collaboration. It could also adapt materials for each learner, ensuring that everyone—whether in rural Africa or a European capital—accesses the same lesson at a level suited to their abilities. In this way, AI would not just connect students; it could level the playing field, offering a shared educational experience regardless of geography.

Such global classrooms could nurture empathy and cultural understanding. Students would not only learn about other cultures from a distance but also learn alongside peers living within those cultures. Discussing climate change with someone directly experiencing rising sea levels, or studying literature with a student for whom the text is part of their national heritage, could transform abstract lessons into lived experiences. This kind of exchange builds not only knowledge but also the global citizenship skills demanded by today's interconnected world.

However, global classrooms also raise complex questions. Whose curriculum would be taught? Education is never just about facts; it reflects values, priorities and perspectives. A global AI-driven classroom risks imposing a dominant narrative, shaped by the most powerful nations or corporations that build the technology. A history lesson, for example, might unintentionally prioritize Western perspectives while overlooking others. Without careful oversight, global classrooms could homogenize education instead of celebrating diversity.

Inequality of access poses another challenge. While AI can theoretically connect everyone, many parts of the world still lack reliable internet, modern devices, or affordable electricity. Global classrooms could become dominated by students from wealthier countries, reinforcing the very divides they aim to bridge. Without deliberate investment in equitable access, the dream of borderless education may remain just that—a dream for some while a reality for others.

There is also the human element. Local teachers provide cultural context, mentorship and personal connection that AI cannot replace. In a global classroom, students may gain exposure to peers worldwide but lose the intimacy of a teacher who understands their community. The challenge is to strike a balance—using AI to facilitate global interaction while grounding students in local educational ecosystems.

Ultimately, AI could enable global classrooms but the outcome depends on intentional design. If built inclusively, with multiple perspectives and equitable access, they could broaden horizons and prepare students for a future where collaboration across borders is essential. If left to market forces alone, however, they may replicate the biases and inequalities already present in the global system. The opportunity is extraordinary: for the first time in history, education could truly become a shared global endeavor. Whether it becomes a story of connection or of dominance will depend on the wisdom of the choices made today.

WILL AI IN EDUCATION STRENGTHEN HUMAN POTENTIAL, OR RISK REDUCING IT TO MEASURABLE OUTPUTS?

The central tension with AI in education is whether it will elevate human potential to new heights or quietly reduce it to what can be tracked, measured and optimized. On the surface, AI promises efficiency and precision. It can identify where students struggle, tailor lessons to individual needs and deliver instant feedback. These are powerful tools that could help more learners succeed. The risk, however, is that in focusing so heavily on what can be quantified, education may lose sight of the immeasurable—the spark of curiosity, the joy of discovery and the development of character and creativity.

Used wisely, AI can strengthen human potential. Imagine a world where every student, no matter where they live or how crowded their classroom, has access to a personal tutor. AI could help them master foundational skills more quickly, freeing time for deeper exploration. It could adapt to different learning styles, ensuring that students who might otherwise fall behind can find their footing. For adults, it could open new paths for lifelong learning, helping people continually grow as industries and societies evolve. In this way, AI does not just deliver content—it unlocks opportunities for more people to thrive.

Yet, the danger lies in letting AI define education too narrowly. Machines excel at measurement: they can track how many problems a student solves, how quickly they improve, or how often they log in. But what about the student who lingers on a problem because they are thinking deeply? What about originality in an essay that breaks the rules? If schools begin to value only what AI can measure, students may be pushed toward conformity and efficiency at the expense of resilience, imagination and wonder. Human potential is more than a data point and reducing it to one would be a mistake.

Another concern is motivation. If students grow up in systems where AI constantly assesses and optimizes their progress, they may come to see education as something external—driven by feedback loops rather than internal curiosity. True potential comes alive when learners pursue questions because they matter, not because they raise a score. Carelessly applied, AI could undermine intrinsic motivation, making education feel like a game of metrics, rather than a journey of growth.

But this outcome is not inevitable. AI can be designed and implemented in ways that expand, rather than narrow, what is valued. It can free teachers from rote tasks so they can nurture curiosity and creativity. It can highlight progress not only in speed and accuracy but also in persistence, collaboration and originality. It can open doors to global perspectives, broadening students' sense of possibility. In short, AI can serve human potential if the immeasurable remains central to education.

The ultimate question is one of intention. If schools and policymakers treat AI as a shortcut to better test scores or higher rankings, it will almost certainly reduce education to outputs. But if AI is embraced as a tool to amplify the human side of learning—our curiosity, empathy, imagination and resilience—it could help cultivate a generation more capable and inspired than any before. The choice does not lie in the technology itself but in how society chooses to wield it.

CONCLUSION

Artificial Intelligence is reshaping education—not by replacing teachers but by reimagining how learning happens.

AI's presence in the classroom is not science fiction; it's already here, enhancing personalized learning, automating administrative tasks and making education more accessible across geographic and socioeconomic boundaries. When implemented thoughtfully, AI can support teachers, empower students and close longstanding gaps in achievement.

But these benefits don't arrive automatically. They depend on how educators, institutions, policymakers and communities choose to engage with the technology. Success will not be measured by how many AI tools we adopt but by how wisely we use them—ensuring that innovation never comes at the expense of equity, privacy or human connection.

The role of the teacher is evolving, not disappearing. In fact, the human element in education becomes more essential in an AI-powered world. Empathy, mentorship, moral guidance and cultural understanding are all things machines cannot replicate. These are the qualities educators must double down on, even as they learn to navigate new digital tools.

AI will continue to advance. The question is: will our education systems evolve with it? If we remain passive, we risk letting algorithms shape learning in ways that serve convenience over quality. But if we lead with vision, ethics and adaptability, we can turn AI into a catalyst for better, more inclusive education.

The future of learning is not AI-driven or human-led. It is both. And it begins now—with awareness, intention and a commitment to shaping education not just for efficiency but for deeper understanding.

DAVID GLACIER

'The Glacier Series on *Asking AI'* is a bold, multi-volume exploration of questions about AI that will define humanity's future. These are questions posed to artificial intelligence, where the AI's response quietly guides the conversation. At the center of this series is not just the evolution of AI but the transformation of humanity itself.

The series is built on a foundational premise—that dialogue with machines, with ourselves and with the systems we inhabit is the most powerful tool we have for navigating uncertainty. Each book presents structured inquiries that raise pressing, often uncomfortable questions. Should AI ever govern? Can a machine inspire? What happens to learning when information is no longer scarce?

Rather than chase technical explanations or speculative extremes, the series keeps its gaze on the human interior—on identity, trust, purpose and the moral frameworks that underlie progress. Each book covers a different theme and collectively they paint a picture of a changing humanitarian landscape.

The Creative Process Behind the Series

The Glacier Series was born from a process of curated questioning. Drawing from thousands of structured interview questions with AI's ChatGPT, author David Glacier pursued a methodical yet deeply personal approach to shaping the series. Each question is treated not as a prompt for a single answer but as an aperture for insight.

Every book in the series emerged through iterative conversations between a human and a machine, crossing disciplines and incorporating the author's own editing of each response. The result is a body of work that resists dogma and instead welcomes ambiguity, always returning to the core human need to ask, to understand and to belong.

The Glacier Series on Asking AI is not a roadmap but a compass. It does not dictate a destination; instead, it reminds readers why the journey matters.

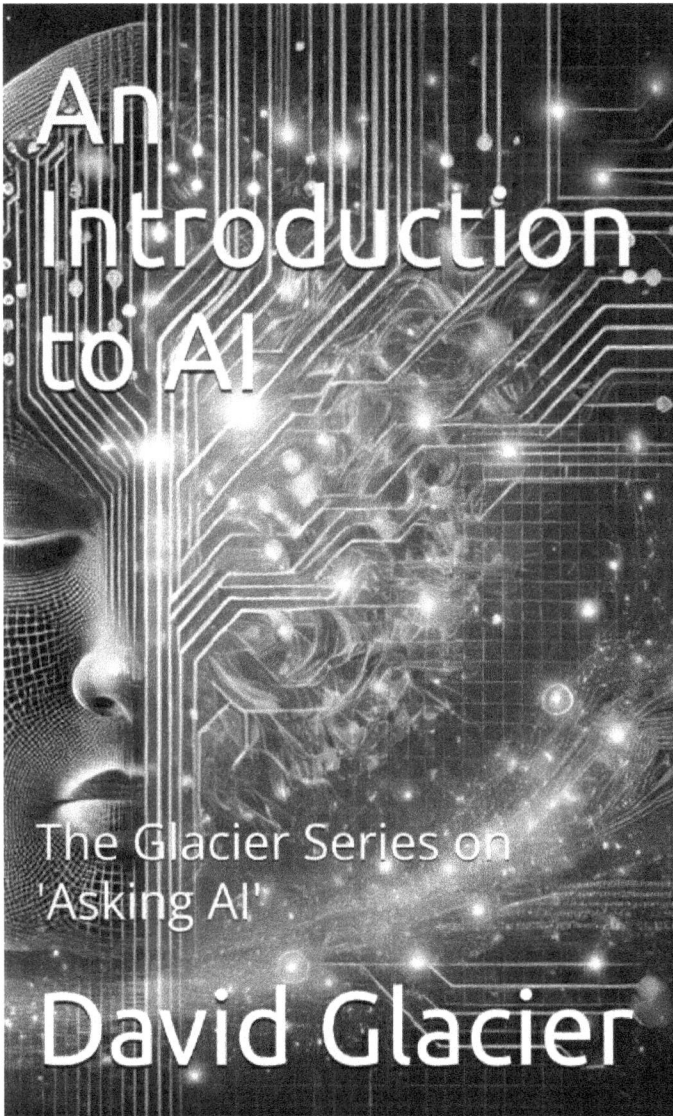

An
Introduction
to AI

The Glacier Series on
'Asking AI'

David Glacier

The Future of AI

The Glacier Series on 'Asking AI'

David Glacier

AI and Creativity

The Glacier Series on 'Asking AI'

David Glacier

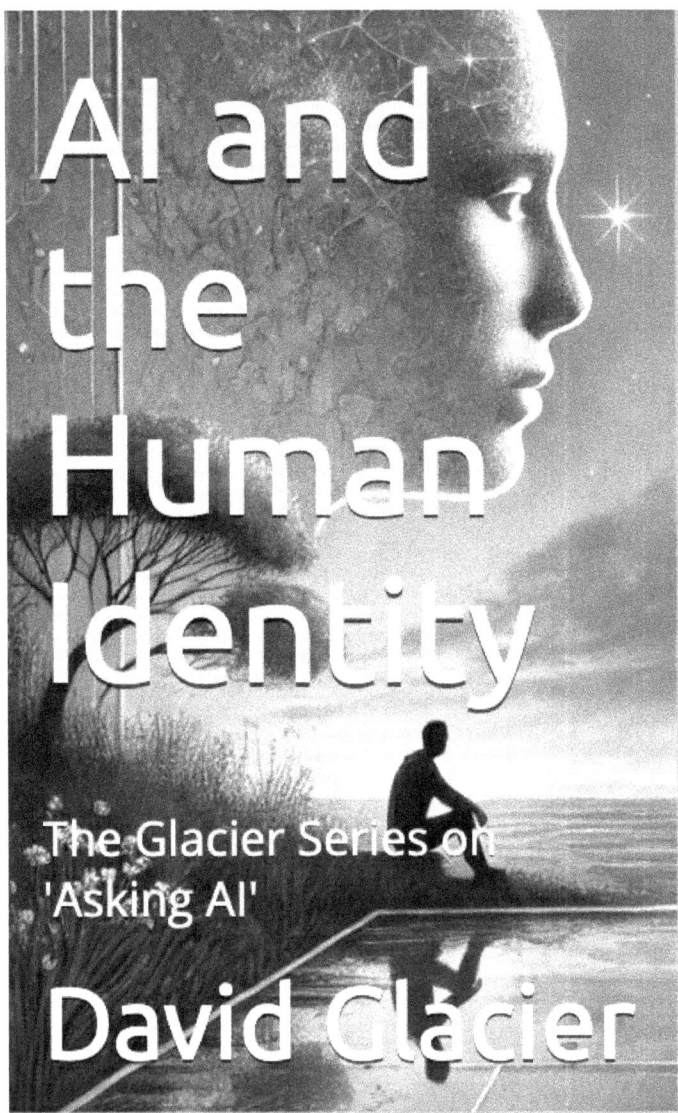

AI and
the
Human
Identity

The Glacier Series on
'Asking AI'

David Glacier

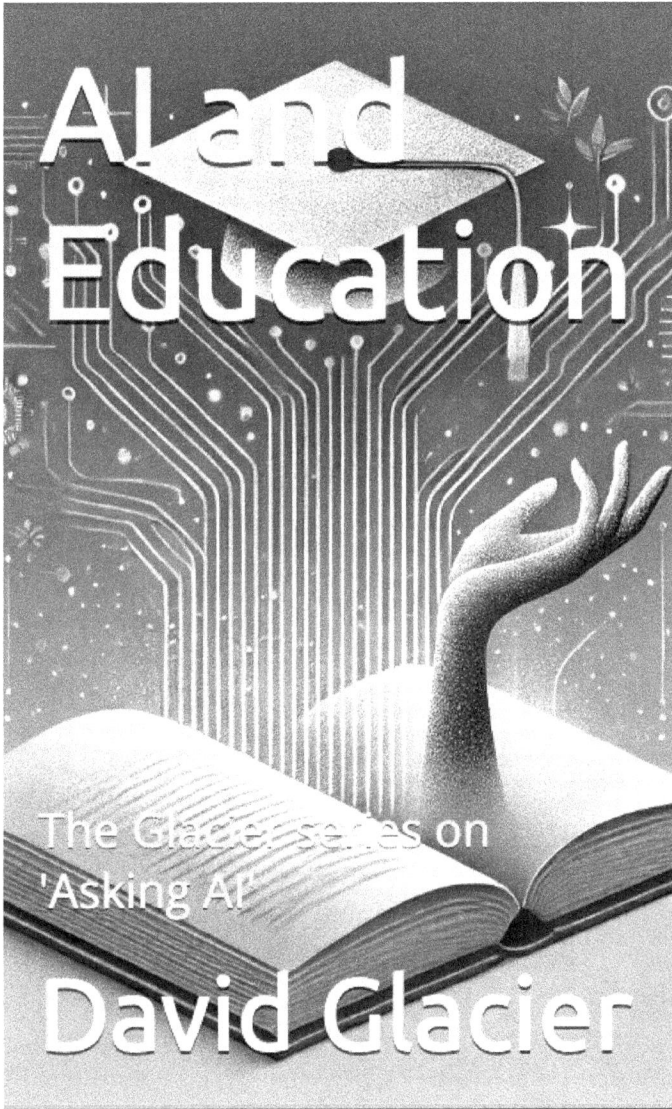

AI and Education

The Glacier series on 'Asking AI'

David Glacier

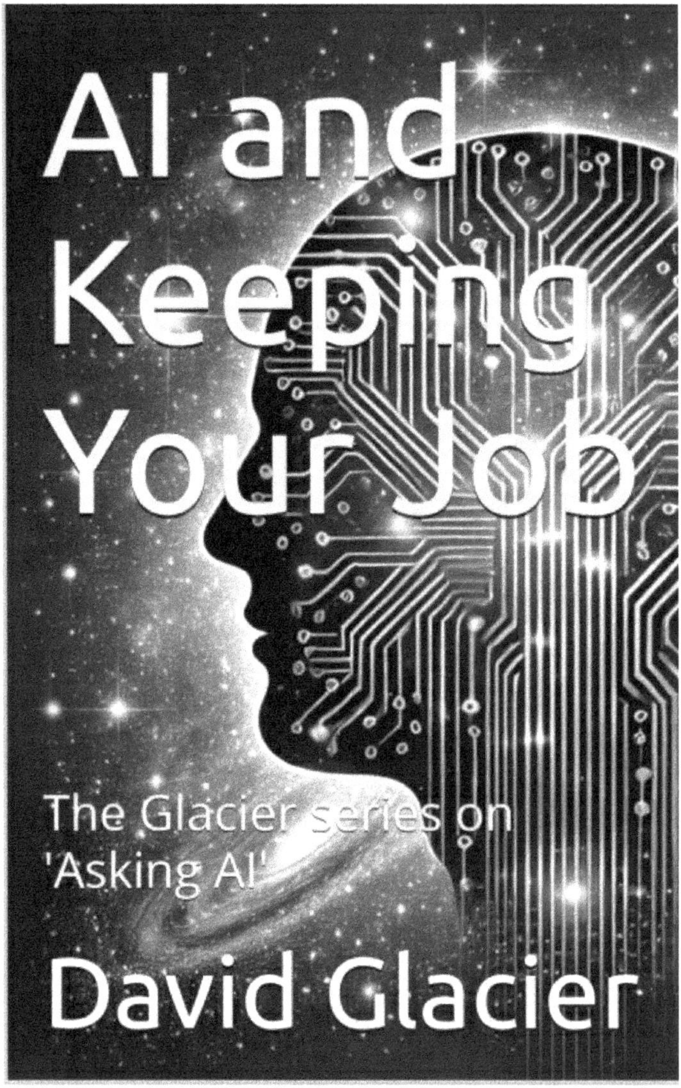
AI and Keeping Your Job
The Glacier series on 'Asking AI'
David Glacier

NOTES

www.ingramcontent.com/pod-product-compliance
Lightning Source LLC
Chambersburg PA
CBHW070942210326
41520CB00021B/7010